W9-AGA-520

To:

From:

TABLE FOR TWO IN

COOKBOOK & MUSIC CD

Michael A. Kornfield

PETER PAUPER PRESS INC.
White Plains, New York

My thanks to Barbara and Brian, my computer consultants;
to Marie-Louise Buret and Sue Milstein, my cooking consultants;
and to Delphine Vaucanson and Elizabeth Poyet
for the Molten Chocolate Cake *recipe*

Designed by Heather Zschock

Visit us at www.peterpauper.com

TABLE FOR TWO IN

Paris

Evening in Paris

On every table Paris spreads a feast
That stirs the senses, bringing fragrance rare
In leafy square and shaded street, from East
To West, through passage lined with flowers fair.

At sunset's rosy glow, the eager throng
With appetite and bold anticipation
Does fill the streets where bistros lie, along
The way to find each culinary station.

As lovers seek a spot where they may spend
The evening lost in one another's gaze,
So Paris, sovereign city sweet, does lend
A hand to love and passion, all ablaze.

Thus food when finely made may play a part
In bringing joy in matters of the heart.

M. A. K.

Contents

———✦✦✦———

Introduction

⌘

*L*overs of fine food, as well as lovers in general, have long identified France with romance and fine cuisine. Is there a secret ingredient in French cooking?

Some say it's the butter and cream. I think it's love, expressed in the care and time taken to select and prepare even the simplest dish. The very act of sitting down to dinner with a close friend or lover, and eating in an unhurried fashion, has been shown to promote a feeling of well-being and intimacy—as well as good digestion. The recipes in this book are mostly for 4 to 6 people, but can be easily modified to prepare a candlelit dinner for two. Many of the dishes are as good the next day, however, so it may not be a bad idea to have some food left over.

I have selected recipes that do not require elaborate equipment. The average French kitchen, like the average American kitchen, is not equipped with the specialized gadgets that are so visible on popular television cooking shows. In fact, all you really need is a little bit of time and the mastery of some basic cooking techniques (not to mention that little pinch of love that every good cook puts into the recipe).

Table for Two in Paris can help you prepare that memorable meal. Create your own version of a Paris bistro by turning down the lights, opening a fine bottle of wine, listening to the romantic CD enclosed, and serving some of the recipes presented in this book.

Vive l'amour et vive la compagnie!

M. A. K.

Tartines de Pistou et Truite Fumé

PESTO AND SMOKED TROUT

Pinch of coarse salt and freshly ground pepper
3 cloves garlic, peeled and crushed
2 cups fresh basil, minced
1 tomato, peeled, seeded and chopped
5 Tbs. olive oil (extra virgin if possible)
12 slices of baguette, toasted
12 thin slices (about 8 oz.) smoked trout

Mix salt, pepper, garlic, and basil with a heavy spoon. Add tomato and mix well. Then add olive oil 1 tablespoon at a time, until the whole mixture has the consistency of a thick mayonnaise. This should produce about 6 tablespoons pesto. Cover each slice of baguette with 1/2 tablespoon of pesto and place one slice of smoked trout on top. May be served as either an hors d'oeuvre or a first course.

6 servings

Artichauts à la Barigoule

ARTICHOKES STUFFED WITH GARLIC AND PARSLEY

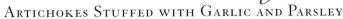

3 artichokes
1/2 tsp. fresh lemon juice
2 cloves garlic
4 sprigs parsley
Salt and freshly ground pepper
2 sprigs fresh thyme
2 Tbs. olive oil
1/4 bottle white wine, approximately

Using a stainless steel knife, remove stalks and tough outer leaves of the artichokes, cut tops almost halfway down, and remove chokes (the inedible centers) with a small spoon. As each artichoke is prepared, place it in a bowl containing 1 teaspoon lemon juice in 1 quart of water (to prevent them from discoloring). Place artichokes upright in a shallow flame-proof earthenware casserole, just large enough to hold them. Chop garlic and parsley, add salt and pepper, and stuff artichoke centers with the mixture. Pour a small amount of olive oil into each artichoke. Season and sprinkle with thyme leaves. Add enough white wine to casserole to come halfway up the sides of artichokes. Cover, and simmer for 1-1/2 hours, removing the lid for the last 10-15 minutes so that most of the wine can evaporate. Sprinkle with additional fresh pepper before serving.

3 servings

Gougères
CHEESE PUFFS

1/4 tsp. salt
1/8 lb. unsalted butter, chilled and cut into small pieces
1/2 cup minus 3/4 Tbs. unbleached all-purpose flour, sifted
2 large eggs
3/8 cup freshly grated imported French Comté or Swiss Gruyère cheese, divided

Preheat oven to 425°. Combine 1/2 cup water, salt, and butter in a medium-size saucepan. Bring to a boil over high heat, stirring steadily with a wooden spoon. Remove pan from heat and add flour. Beat with a large wooden spoon to create a smooth dough. Reheat for 1 minute over medium heat, stirring all the time, to allow dough to dry out somewhat. Quickly transfer dough to a mixer bowl. Add eggs and half the grated cheese, and beat with electric mixer at medium speed until eggs and cheese are well blended into the dough mixture. The dough should still be warm. With a tablespoon, place 2-inch mounds of dough on nonstick baking sheet, spacing them about 2 inches apart. Sprinkle tops with remaining grated cheese. Bake 12 to 15 minutes until puffs are golden brown.

About 20 cheese puffs

Tapenade
Olive Paste

8 oz. French-style black olives, pitted (Olives in oil and with Herbes de Provence are
available in most markets.)
2 salt anchovies, rinsed and filleted, or 4 canned fillets, drained
3 Tbs. capers
1 garlic clove, peeled and thoroughly crushed, with a pinch of coarse salt
Small pinch of cayenne
1 tsp. fresh savory leaves, finely chopped, or a pinch of crumbled dried savory leaves
4 Tbs. extra virgin olive oil

In a food processor, mix the olives, anchovies, capers, garlic, cayenne, and savory to a coarse purée. Add olive oil and process until the mixture is smooth and uniform in texture. This should only take a few moments. The tapenade is a delicious spread on toast rounds or unsalted crackers.

1-1/2 cups

Crevettes Louisianne

LOUISIANA SHRIMP

3/8 cup olive oil, divided
1-2 cloves garlic, minced
1/2 medium onion, minced
1 lb. medium shrimp, shelled and deveined
3 scallions including green part, minced
1/4 cup red wine vinegar
1/2 tsp. salt
1/4 tsp. pepper
1/2 tsp. dry mustard
1/8 tsp. cayenne pepper

Heat 1/8 cup oil in a heavy skillet. Add garlic and minced onion and cook over moderate heat for 10 minutes, stirring constantly. Add shrimp and sauté, stirring constantly, 5-7 minutes. Remove from stove and allow to cool. In a large bowl, prepare the marinade with the remaining oil, minced scallions, vinegar, and seasonings. Add shrimp mixture.

Refrigerate covered overnight before serving, to allow the flavors to blend thoroughly.

6 servings

Pâté aux Foies de Volaille

CHICKEN LIVER PÂTÉ

2 Tbs. butter
1 lb. chicken livers, whole
2 Tbs. flour
1/2 cup dry white wine
2 shallots, minced
2 garlic cloves, crushed
2 Tbs. cognac

1/2 lb. boiled ham, diced
pinch nutmeg
1 tsp. salt
1/4 tsp. pepper
1/2 lb. bacon
1 large bay leaf

Preheat oven to 475°. Melt butter in a sauté pan and sauté chicken livers for 8-10 minutes, mixing as they cook. Add flour to cooked livers, using large spoon to distribute flour evenly, and cook at moderate heat for a minute or two. In a large bowl, mix wine, shallots, garlic, cognac, ham, nutmeg, salt, and pepper. Add chicken livers to bowl and mash with large fork. Line a 10-inch to 12-inch terrine pan or other oval dish with bacon strips, covering bottom first. Then add mixture to pan, spreading it evenly. Place a bay leaf on top, cover, and place in center of oven. Cook for 1-1/2 hours. Remove casserole from oven and let cool. Refrigerate overnight if possible. Cut around edges of paté with a sharp knife and remove carefully.

8-10 servings

Quiche Lorraine

DOUGH:
1 cup flour
Pinch of salt
1/3 cup butter
1 Tbs. vegetable shortening
FILLING:
1 Tbs. butter
1 lb. peeled sweet onions, cut in half and
  sliced

2 eggs, beaten
1/2 cup grated Gruyère cheese
2/3 cup light cream
1/2 tsp. dried mustard
2 thick slices (approx. 1/2 lb.) boiled ham,
  cubed
Salt and pepper

Preheat oven to 350°.

DOUGH: Sift flour and salt into a bowl. Cut butter and shortening into small pieces and drop them into flour, using fingers to mix completely. Mix to a firm but pliable dough with a few tablespoons cold water. Knead until smooth. Cover lightly and chill for 15 minutes in refrigerator. Roll out on a lightly floured board and use to line a 9-inch pie pan.

FILLING: Melt butter in a frying pan and add onions. Cook slowly, until they turn a light golden-brown color. Place in a bowl. Add beaten eggs, cheese, cream, mustard, ham, and salt and pepper to taste, and mix well. Pour into prepared pastry shell. Bake in preheated oven for 20-25 minutes until golden brown. Serve hot or cold.

6-8 servings

NOTE: May be used as a main course if desired.

Soupe à l'Oignon
ONION SOUP

3 Tbs. butter
5 medium onions (about 2 lbs.), thinly sliced
1 Tbs. flour
1/2 tsp. salt
Freshly ground black pepper
5 cups beef broth
4 thick slices French or Italian bread
1 cup grated Swiss or Gruyère cheese, or French Comté

Melt butter in a heavy pan. Add sliced onions and cook slowly, until golden, stirring occasionally. Sprinkle on flour and continue to cook, stirring, for a few minutes. Season with salt and pepper. Add broth, stirring constantly. Bring to a boil, then lower heat and let soup simmer, partially covered, for 30 minutes. Toast bread slices in the oven until brown. Place them in large flameproof baking dish. Sprinkle toast with cheese. Melt cheese under the broiler and place each slice in a bowl of soup.

4 servings

Soupe au Pistou
VEGETABLE SOUP WITH PESTO

4 oz. dried kidney beans

4 oz. dried white beans

1 bay leaf

1 lamb or veal shank

1 Tbs. coarse or sea salt

Pinch cayenne pepper

2 carrots, peeled and diced

1/2 lb. onion, peeled and sliced

3 potatoes, peeled, cut into quarters, and
   sliced

3 tomatoes, peeled, seeded and quartered

1 lb. Hubbard, acorn, or pumpkin squash,
   seeded, peeled, and diced

1 lb. zucchini, trimmed and cut into quarters
   and then into 3/4-inch slices

1/2 lb. green beans, trimmed and cut to
   1-inch length

5 cloves garlic, peeled and crushed

1 cup small elbow macaroni

1 recipe Pistou (see p. 11)

Freshly grated Gruyère or Parmesan cheese
   for serving

Soak beans overnight in 1 quart water. Next morning, drain, and add beans and bay leaf to 2 quarts cold water. Bring to a boil over moderate heat and simmer for 15 minutes. Drain beans and reserve. In the meantime, place lamb or veal shank into a large enameled ironware pot in 3 quarts water, and bring slowly to a boil, skimming off gray scum from surface. Boil meat for 15-20 minutes. Add salt, cayenne, all soup vegetables, and garlic. Return to a boil and add beans. Adjust heat to maintain a simmer, with pot partly covered, for about 2 hours. Leave uncovered to cool. Remove lamb or veal shank, separate flesh from the bone, cut meat into small pieces, and add them to soup. In the evening, reheat soup. When soup reaches a boil, add macaroni and cook at a light boil for 12-15 minutes. If soup seems too thick (it should be thick), add a bit of boiling water and taste for salt.

Remove soup pot from heat, and stir pistou into the soup (wash out mixing bowl with a ladle of soup and pour it back into pot). Serve directly from the soup pot accompanied by a dish of grated cheese.

8 servings

Potage Saint-Germain

PEA SOUP

1 head Boston lettuce
2 lbs. unshelled peas or 10 oz. frozen peas
1/4 lb. butter
1/2 tsp. salt
1 tsp. sugar
Freshly ground black pepper

Wash lettuce and shred leaves into strips. Shell peas if using fresh peas. Melt butter in a saucepan. Add lettuce, shelled peas, salt, and sugar. Cover and simmer over low heat for 10 minutes. Add 4 cups water and simmer another 10 minutes until peas are tender. Purée soup in blender. Return to a clean saucepan. Add pepper. Bring soup to a simmer. Serve hot.

6 servings

Potage Parmentier

Leek and Potato Soup

5 potatoes, peeled and sliced
3 leeks (about 1 lb.), washed and thinly sliced (use white part only)
1/2 quart water or chicken broth
1/2 tsp. marjoram
1 Tbs. salt (omit if using chicken broth)
2-3 oz. heavy cream (optional)
3 Tbs. fresh parsley, minced

Simmer potatoes and leeks in water, add marjoram and salt, and cook, partly covered, for 50 minutes, until tender. Either put soup through a food mill or mash with fork or potato masher. Before serving, add 2-3 oz. heavy cream, if desired. Decorate with fresh parsley.

4 servings

Tomates à la Languedocienne

TOMATOES, LANGUEDOC STYLE

4 large ripe tomatoes
1 Tbs. olive oil
1 clove garlic, crushed
4 large slices French country bread
1 Tbs. fresh parsley, chopped
2 tsp. thyme or marjoram, chopped
Salt and pepper

Preheat oven to 350°. Cut tomatoes in half and score the cut surface. Sprinkle with salt and leave upside-down in a colander to drain for 1-2 hours. Rinse tomatoes and scoop out most of the juice and pulp. Mix olive oil and garlic together and brush both sides of bread with mixture, leaving bread to soften. Chop herbs and bread together until well mixed. Press filling into tomatoes and sprinkle with any remaining garlic and olive oil mixture. Cook tomatoes in a flameproof dish in preheated oven for 5 minutes. Brown tomatoes under broiler for another 2-3 minutes. Serve immediately.

4 servings

Tourte aux Asperges

ASPARAGUS TART

1 qt. ice water
2 unbaked pie crusts, chilled
1-1/2 lbs. asparagus, trimmed
1 Tbs. olive oil
6 oz. boiled ham, minced
1 large sweet onion, peeled, cut in half, and thinly sliced
1 Tbs. unbleached all purpose flour
Salt and freshly ground black pepper
1 egg
Zest of 1 lemon, minced (optional)
2 cups grated Gruyère or Comté cheese, divided

Cook asparagus in a large pot of salted boiling water for 2-4 minutes, until bright green. Place asparagus in a large bowl filled with ice water for a few minutes. Keep 1 cup of cooking liquid for later use. Dry asparagus with paper towels after it has cooled. Heat oil in a large heavy saucepan over medium-high heat, and add ham and onion. Cook just until golden, about 5 minutes. Sprinkle flour over ham and onions, and stir. Stir in 1/4 cup reserved asparagus cooking liquid. Cook, stirring constantly, until liquid thickens and flour is cooked, at least 2 minutes. Add remaining 3/4 cup cooking liquid, stirring and scraping bottom of pan. Cook until mixture has thickened to consistency of mayonnaise, about 5 minutes. Season to taste with salt and pepper. Remove pan from heat and let mixture cool to lukewarm. (The recipe can be made up to this point several hours in advance.)

Preheat oven to 400°. Whisk egg and 2 teaspoons water together to make an egg wash. Cut tips from asparagus stalks; cut remaining stalks into 2-inch lengths. Stir lemon zest (if desired) into ham and onion mixture and mix thoroughly. Press one chilled pie crust into 9-inch pie pan. Spread half ham and onion mixture as evenly as possible in crust, top with half the asparagus, and sprinkle evenly with half the cheese. Then spread a layer of the remaining ham and onion mixture, top with remaining asparagus, and sprinkle with remaining cheese. Place top pie crust over filling and press together with bottom crust at the edges. Trim sides and then spread egg wash with a pastry brush over all exposed parts of crust, and pierce crust several times with a sharp knife to allow steam to escape. Bake tourte in the center of preheated oven until crust is golden on top, about 30 minutes. Remove tourte from oven. Let cool for 10 to 20 minutes before serving.

6-8 servings

Épinards au Muscade

SPINACH WITH NUTMEG

1 lb. spinach, trimmed and washed
1 Tbs. butter
1 Tbs. olive oil
1/4 tsp. salt
1/8 tsp. pepper
1/4 tsp. nutmeg

Immerse spinach in a bowl of cold water, lift out spinach and place it in another bowl. Heat butter and olive oil in a large frying pan over high heat and add half the spinach. Cook until spinach starts to wilt; then add reserved spinach and cover pan. Continue cooking for a minute, remove lid and add remaining ingredients, stirring thoroughly. Cook over high heat for another 3-4 minutes, or until most of the liquid has evaporated. Serve immediately.

4 servings

Les Haricots Verts et Pommes Gratinées

GRATIN OF GREEN BEANS AND POTATOES

1/2 lb. potatoes, peeled and sliced
3 garlic cloves, chopped fine
1/2 lb. green beans, washed and trimmed and
   cut into 1-inch pieces

SAUCE:
1/4 cup butter
2 Tbs. whole-wheat flour
2/3 cup vegetable stock
2/3 cup light cream
1 cup Gruyère or Comté cheese, grated
Sea salt and freshly ground black pepper

Place potatoes and garlic in a pan with 5 cups water and boil until tender, about 20-25 minutes. Cook green beans separately in boiling water for 6-8 minutes. Drain vegetables, reserving 2/3 cup of liquid for the sauce. Combine vegetables in a shallow earthenware baking dish and set aside.

To make the sauce, heat butter in a saucepan and stir in flour. Cook on low heat, stirring to form a roux. Do not allow to brown. Gradually add vegetable stock, stirring all the time, to make a smooth mixture; then slowly add cream. Mix in half the cheese and season to taste with salt and pepper. Cover vegetables with sauce, then sprinkle remaining cheese over the top. Place under a hot broiler until golden brown. Serve immediately.

4 servings

Asperges et Morilles

ASPARAGUS AND MUSHROOMS

2 Tbs. white wine vinegar
1-1/4 lbs. asparagus
1/4 cup butter
1/2 lb. morels or cultivated mushrooms, cleaned and sliced
Salt and pepper to taste
2 Tbs. parsley, chopped
2 Tbs. fresh lemon juice

Add vinegar to boiling water, and cook asparagus until it is bright green and a fork can be inserted with moderate resistance. Drain and transfer to a serving plate and keep warm. Place butter in a skillet and stir-fry mushrooms for 3-4 minutes over high heat. Scatter salt and pepper and parsley over mushrooms. Mix asparagus and mushrooms together. Sprinkle with lemon juice, pour pan juices over, and serve.

6 servings

Ratatouille

VEGETABLE STEW, MEDITERRANEAN STYLE

1/2 lb. eggplant, cut into 1-inch cubes
3/4-1 Tbs. coarse salt
3 Tbs. olive oil
1/2 lb. sweet onions, halved and thinly sliced
3 oz. dry white wine, such as Macon blanc
1/2 lb. zucchini, quartered and cut into 3/4-inch sections
1/2 lb. tomatoes, peeled, seeded and quartered
1-1/2 sweet peppers, seeded and cut into long strips
3 cloves garlic, peeled and crushed
1/2 tsp. salt
1/4 tsp. pepper
Bouquet garni (2 bay leaves and 3 sprigs fresh thyme in cheesecloth)

Place eggplant in a colander. Sprinkle with coarse salt and let eggplant drain for 30 minutes. Wash eggplant and pat dry. Heat oil in a large casserole and sauté eggplant for 5-10 minutes. Add onions and sauté for another 5-10 minutes until onions are translucent. Add wine and remaining vegetables. Turn heat down and add garlic, salt, and pepper, stirring well. Add bouquet garni and mix well again. Simmer uncovered for 50-60 minutes. Remove bouquet garni. (Ratatouille will taste even better if you let it cool and sit overnight in the refrigerator. It is delicious cold or can be reheated the next day.)

4-5 servings

Soufflé de Pommes de Terre

POTATO SOUFFLÉ

1-1/2 lbs. potatoes, peeled and quartered
Salt
5 Tbs. butter
1 cup whole milk, heated
1/4 tsp. pepper
1/8 tsp. nutmeg
1/2 cup freshly grated Parmesan or Gruyère cheese
3 eggs, separated
1 egg yolk, beaten with a fork

Preheat oven to 400°. Boil potatoes in salted water until just done, about 30 minutes. Drain potatoes and mash thoroughly with a potato masher. Stir in 5 tablespoons butter, cut into small pieces, and add heated milk, to make a fairly loose purée. Salt to taste. Add pepper and nutmeg and mix in cheese. Beat 3 egg yolks with a fork and stir them in. Whisk egg whites with a pinch of salt until they form soft peaks, and fold them in gently with a wooden spoon. Empty mixture into a generously buttered dish and, with a pastry brush, paint the surface lightly with other beaten egg yolk. Bake for 20-25 minutes, or until golden brown. Serve immediately.

6 generous servings

Gratin Dauphinois

Potato Gratin

1 garlic clove, cut in half
2 lbs. baking potatoes, peeled and thinly sliced
1 cup freshly grated French Comté or Swiss Gruyère cheese
1 cup crème fraîche or heavy cream

Preheat oven to 350°. Thoroughly rub a shallow, 6-cup oval baking dish with garlic. Layer half of potatoes in dish. Sprinkle with half of cheese and then half of crème fraîche or heavy cream. Sprinkle with salt. Add another layer of potatoes, cheese, and crème fraîche or cream. Bake, uncovered, until gratin is crisp and golden on top, 50-60 minutes. Serve immediately.

4 servings

Sauce Hollandaise

HOLLANDAISE SAUCE

3 egg yolks
1 tsp. lemon juice
Salt and pepper to taste
1/2 lb. butter

Place egg yolks, lemon juice and a pinch of salt and pepper with 1 teaspoon water in a saucepan. Beat ingredients with a wire whisk over low heat for 4 or 5 minutes, until sauce appears creamy. If the sauce becomes foamy, raise heat under pan a little bit. Do not raise heat too much or you will have scrambled eggs. Add butter in small pieces one at a time. The sauce will be ready when the mixture thickens to a creamy texture.

Rouille

GARLIC, SAFFRON, AND PEPPER MAYONNAISE

6 large fresh garlic cloves
Salt
2 large egg yolks, at room temperature
1 cup extra-virgin olive oil
1/4 tsp. saffron threads
Pinch cayenne pepper

Peel and cut garlic cloves in half and remove the green, sprout-like "germs" that run lengthwise through the center of garlic. Pour boiling water into a large mortar to warm it; discard water, and dry mortar. Place garlic in mortar, add a pinch of salt, and mash evenly with a pestle to form a paste. Add 1 egg yolk. Stir, pressing slowly and evenly with the pestle, always in the same direction, to thoroughly blend the garlic and yolk. Add second yolk and repeat until well blended. Very slowly work in oil, drop by drop, until the mixture thickens. After you have added a few drops of oil, add saffron and a pinch of cayenne. Gradually whisk in remaining oil in a slow, thin stream until sauce is thickened to a mayonnaise consistency. Taste the rouille and add additional cayenne, if desired. Cover and refrigerate until ready to serve.

About 1-1/4 cups

Sauce Béarnaise

BÉARNAISE SAUCE

1/4 cup white or red wine vinegar
1/4 cup dry white wine
1-1/2 Tbs. minced shallots
3 Tbs. minced fresh tarragon, divided
Pinch salt
1/8 tsp. pepper
3 egg yolks
2 Tbs. cold butter
8 Tbs. melted butter

Place vinegar, wine, shallots, 1 tablespoon tarragon, and salt and pepper in a small saucepan and bring to a boil. Reduce total volume to 2 tablespoons and allow it to cool. Beat egg yolks until thickened. Pour the cooled vinegar mixture through a strainer into the bowl containing egg yolks. Beat again and add 1 tablespoon cold butter. Place pan over low heat, beating continuously to thicken the egg yolks further. Add second tablespoon cold butter and beat it into the mixture. Add melted butter very slowly while continuing to beat. Remove pan from heat and mix in remaining tarragon.

1-1/2 cups

Poisson à la Niçoise

FISH FILLETS NIÇOISE

3/4 cup finely chopped onions
6 small fish fillets (about 4 oz. each)
1 cup peeled, seeded, and diced tomatoes
1-1/2 tsp. salt
3/4 cup dry white wine
1/4 cup (1/2 stick) butter

Preheat oven to 400°. Wash chopped onions in a sieve under cold water. Press to remove excess water. Arrange fillets, skin side up, in a large baking dish and cover with onions and tomatoes. Add remaining ingredients, except butter. Place a piece of buttered waxed paper on top and bake in center of preheated oven for 10-12 minutes. Remove fish and keep warm on a covered platter. Pour the juice into a saucepan and reduce juice to about 2/3 cup. Add butter, piece by piece, beating with a whisk. Boil mixture for a minute or two, pour over fish, and serve.

4 servings

Bouillabaisse

Marseilles Fish Stew

1 lb. swordfish or monkfish	Salt
1 lb. halibut	3-4 small red potatoes, scrubbed
1 lb. flounder or sole	1/8 tsp. saffron threads
1/4 cup extra virgin olive oil	Bay leaf
1 lb. fresh ripe tomatoes, cored and quartered	1/4 tsp. thyme
1/2 lb. onions, quartered	1/4 tsp. dried orange peel
3 fresh garlic cloves, peeled and crushed	1/8 tsp. pepper
1 fennel bulb, trimmed and quartered	Baguette rounds, toasted
1 bunch fresh parsley, washed and dried	Rouille (see p. 36)
1/2 cup sliced leeks	

Fillet all whole fish, and reserve heads and tails for stock. Cut larger fillets and steaks into 1-inch thick pieces. Carefully remove any remaining scales and gills, which might turn the stock bitter. Rinse and pat dry all fish and refrigerate until needed.

This step may be done several hours ahead of serving, if desired. Bring a large kettle of water to boil. Heat oil over medium-high heat until hot but not smoking, in a heavy non-reactive 12-quart stockpot. Add tomatoes, onions, garlic, fennel, and parsley, and cook about 5 minutes, uncovered, over medium-high heat, just until mixture begins to soften. Add cooked vegetables and all fish trimmings to stockpot. Add enough boiling water (about 2-3 quarts) to cover ingredients. Add salt to taste, cover, and allow to boil vigorously until broth is orange red and just moderately thick, about 45 minutes. Strain soup into a bowl. Discard the solids. You should have 1 to 1-1/2 quarts fish soup.

Steam or boil potatoes until tender. Set aside and keep warm. Return fish soup to the stockpot; add saffron, bay leaf, thyme, orange peel, and pepper. Bring to a boil over high heat. Add fish fillets and pieces to the soup—the swordfish or monkfish first, the other fish varieties about 5 minutes later—and cook just until fish are cooked through but still firm, a total of 10-12 minutes. To serve, slice potatoes and place them on bottom of warmed soup bowls. Place 3 pieces fish on top of potatoes in each bowl, and pour warm broth over all. Serve with toasted baguette slices and rouille.

3 to 4 servings

FILLET OF SOLE BERCY

1-3/4 lbs. sole or flounder fillets, skinless
1/2 tsp. salt
Freshly ground black pepper
4 scallions, finely chopped
2 Tbs. parsley, finely chopped
1/2 cup white wine
2 Tbs. butter

Preheat oven to 350°. Season fish with salt and pepper. Butter a large oval baking dish. Add scallions, parsley, and wine and place dish in preheated oven for 5 minutes. Take the dish out of oven, arrange fillets in a single layer in dish, and top with pats of butter. Cover fish with aluminum foil and place in oven for 15 minutes. Remove foil and drain off poaching liquid. Place under broiler for 1-2 minutes. Serve hot.

4 servings

Poulet Sauté aux Échalottes

CHICKEN WITH SHALLOTS

3 Tbs. butter
1 Tbs. olive oil
3-4 lb. roasting chicken, cut in pieces
1 tsp. salt

1/4 tsp. pepper
4 shallots, minced
2 cups dry white wine

In a flameproof casserole or Dutch oven, melt butter and add oil. Sear chicken pieces, skin side down, for 3-4 minutes; then turn over and sear for 1-2 minutes. Remove chicken from casserole and season with salt and pepper. Place shallots in casserole and cook 1-2 minutes over moderate heat until softened. Add white wine and mix thoroughly, scraping browned pieces from bottom of casserole. Return chicken to casserole, heat sauce to boiling, and immediately reduce heat to medium and cover casserole. Cook 30 minutes; remove chicken pieces from pan and keep them warm. Boil sauce to reduce volume by about one-third and replace chicken in casserole.

4 servings

Note: This dish may be prepared ahead of time and reheated.

Poulet Sauté Vallée d'Auge

CHICKEN NORMANDY STYLE

2 Tbs. butter, divided
2 Tbs. oil
3-lb. chicken, cut into 8 pieces
4 Tbs. Calvados
1/3 cup chicken stock
2 apples, peeled, cored, and coarsely chopped
2 shallots, finely chopped
2 stalks celery, finely chopped
1/2 tsp. dried thyme

1/3 cup heavy cream
2 egg yolks, lightly beaten
Salt and white pepper

GARNISH
2 Tbs. butter
2 apples, quartered, cored, and cut into cubes
Sugar
1 bunch watercress or small parsley sprigs

Melt butter with the oil in a large sauté pan over moderate heat. Add chicken and brown, skin side down, for 3-4 minutes. Turn pieces over and brown for 2-3 minutes. Remove chicken from pan, pour off most of fat, and replace chicken in pan. Heat Calvados in a small saucepan and light it. Pour Calvados over chicken and let flames die down. Pour stock over chicken and scrape any browned chicken juices from bottom of pan. Set pan aside. Melt remaining butter in a small saucepan and add chopped apples, shallots, celery, and thyme. Cook for about 10 minutes or until soft. Spoon apple mixture over chicken and return pan to high heat. Bring to a boil, then reduce heat, cover pan, and simmer 50 minutes. When chicken is cooked, beat cream and egg yolks together. Add a few tablespoons hot sauce slowly to egg and cream mixture and mix with a wire whisk until a smooth consistency is achieved. Pour mixture back into a saucepan and cook over low heat for 2-3 minutes, stirring constantly until sauce thickens. Season sauce with salt and white pepper and set aside while preparing garnish. Melt remaining butter in a small frying pan and add apples. Toss over high heat until apples are soft. Sprinkle with sugar and cook a few more minutes. To serve, coat chicken with sauce and decorate with watercress or parsley. Spoon caramelized apples over chicken.

6 servings

Poulet au Vinaigre de Framboise

RASPBERRY CHICKEN

———⟋⟍⟋⟍———

3-4 lb. roasting chicken
Salt and pepper
1 Tbs. oil
5 Tbs. butter, divided

4 medium sized shallots, finely chopped
1/2 cup raspberry vinegar, preferably
   imported from France
1 cup heavy cream

Preheat oven to 400°. Cut chicken into 8 pieces, by removing drumsticks from legs at the joint (4 pieces) and by cutting each half breast in two (4 pieces). Wash each piece of chicken and dry thoroughly. Season each piece of chicken with salt and pepper. Put oil and 3 tablespoons butter in a large skillet over medium high heat. When butter is melted and hot, add pieces of chicken skin-side down. Let chicken cook for about 3 minutes or until golden brown. Turn pieces over and cook about 1 minute more. Turn pieces of chicken back to skin side and place skillet in preheated oven for 10 minutes. Remove breast pieces and cook thighs and legs for another 6-8 minutes. Remove thighs and legs from skillet and keep all pieces warm. Pour off 2/3 of liquid from pan and discard. Add chopped shallots to remaining liquid and cook slowly for 1 minute, stirring constantly. Add raspberry vinegar and cook for another 3 minutes, until quantity is reduced by half. Stir in heavy cream and cook slowly for another 2-3 minutes. Stir in remaining 2 tablespoons butter and season to taste. (The sauce should have a mild bite.) Strain sauce over chicken and serve.

4 servings

Coq au Vin

CHICKEN WITH WINE

1/2 lb. bacon

1 Tbs. butter

2 Tbs. olive oil, divided

1/2 lb. carrots, sliced

20 small white onions

1/2 lb. mushrooms, cut in quarters

4 lb. chicken, cut into 8 pieces

3/4-1 tsp. salt

Freshly ground pepper

2 Tbs. brandy, warmed in a flameproof pan

2 tomatoes, peeled, seeded, and coarsely
   chopped

3 Tbs. flour

2 cups red wine

1/2 tsp. thyme

2 bay leaves

1 Tbs. finely chopped parsley

Sauté bacon in a large flameproof casserole until the fat is rendered. Remove bacon from pan and drain, discarding bacon fat. Combine butter and 1 tablespoon oil in pan, add carrots and onions, and cook until onions are slightly colored, about 5 minutes. Remove vegetables and reserve. Sauté mushrooms in one tablespoon olive oil. Brown chicken on both sides, adding additional oil if necessary. Sprinkle chicken pieces with salt and pepper. Light brandy and pour over chicken. After flame dies down, add tomatoes and cook 3 minutes. Return bacon, onions, and carrots to casserole and add mushrooms. Add flour and cook 2-3 minutes, stirring constantly. Add wine and bring to a boil. Reduce heat to medium and add remaining ingredients. Cover pot and simmer for 35-40 minutes. Remove bay leaves before serving.

6 servings

Porc aux Pruneaux

PORK WITH PRUNES

Salt and freshly ground pepper
3 lb. boned pork loin
2 Tbs. oil
20-24 pitted prunes, soaked in 6 oz. red wine
   for 1 hour

2 Tbs. finely chopped shallots
3 Tbs. Cognac or Armagnac
1 cup red wine for sauce

Preheat oven to 400°. Salt and pepper pork. Oil base of a roasting pan and place pork in pan. Roast in oven for 1-1/4 hours. Meanwhile, in a saucepan bring the prunes and wine to a boil. Reduce heat and simmer for 15 minutes. Turn off heat. About 15 minutes before meat is fully roasted, pour prune and wine mixture around the pork in pan. When pork is cooked, remove from oven and place on a platter. Remove as much fat from pan as possible. Place pan over high heat. Add shallots and sauté for a minute or two. Return meat to roasting pan. Pour brandy into a small saucepan, heat it over moderate heat, and set it aflame. Pour flaming brandy over roast and let flames die down. Then return meat to the platter. Add remaining wine to roasting pan and stir while bringing mixture to a boil, scraping bottom of pan. Season with salt and pepper. Transfer meat to a warmed serving dish and arrange prunes around meat. Strain gravy and pour over meat.

4-6 servings

Filet Mignon

Basic Filet Mignon

1 Tbs. butter
2 beef filet steaks, about 3" diameter and 1" thick (about 6 oz. each)
2 oz. veal or beef stock

Melt butter in sauté pan over medium high heat and sauté steaks 3-4 minutes on each side. Remove steaks from pan and add stock, stirring to incorporate the little bits that stick to the pan. Pour sauce over meat and serve immediately.

2 servings

Filet Mignon with Sauce Béarnaise

Prepare the Sauce Béarnaise according to the recipe on p. 37. Sauté filets as in the master recipe, omitting the stock. Serve with a generous spoonful of Béarnaise sauce on top of each filet.

Grilled Filet Mignon

1 Tbs. oil
2 filet steaks, about 6 oz. each
Pepper

1/2 to 1 tsp. Herbes de Provence
1 to 1-1/2 Tbs. Maître d'Hôtel butter (see
  below)

Brush the oil on the steaks and season with pepper and Herbes de Provence. Grill under a broiler 5-6 minutes on each side. Serve with a slice of Maître d'Hôtel butter on top of each steak.

2 servings

Maître d'Hôtel Butter

3/4 cup butter
1/2 tsp. salt
1/8 tsp. pepper

1 Tbs. fresh lemon juice
1 Tbs. chopped parsley

Let butter soften at room temperature and make into a paste with a large spoon. Add the other ingredients and blend thoroughly. This will keep for three days in the refrigerator.

Sauté de Veau aux Carottes

VEAL STEW WITH CARROTS

1/4 cup extra virgin olive oil
2 lbs. boneless stewing veal, cut into large (2 oz.) cubes
Salt and freshly ground black pepper
2 onions, cut into thin rounds
1 bottle white wine, such as Muscadet, divided
3 imported bay leaves
2 tsp. Herbes de Provence
2 small tomatoes, cored, peeled, seeded, and chopped
2 lbs. tender young carrots, peeled and cut into thin rounds

Heat oil in a deep-sided 12-inch skillet over medium-high heat. When oil is hot, brown the cubes of veal on all sides. Season with salt and pepper. Add onions and cook over medium-high heat until onions are soft and translucent, 2-3 minutes. Reduce heat to medium; add 1 cup of wine. Scrape bottom of skillet and mix well. Stir in bay leaves, herbs, and tomatoes. Cover, bring to a simmer, and simmer for about 5 minutes. Pour in 1 more cup of wine. Cover and simmer very gently, over low to medium heat, for 1 hour. Stir in remaining wine. Cover and simmer for 1 more hour. Remove veal from pan and set aside. Add carrots to the skillet. Cover and simmer until soft, 40-45 minutes, by which point carrots will have absorbed much of sauce. Return veal to skillet and reheat until warmed through. Serve immediately.

4 servings

Boeuf à la Mode

BEEF BRAISED IN WINE

8 carrots, thinly sliced
4 onions, finely chopped, divided
1 bay leaf
1/2 tsp. thyme
3 sprigs parsley
1/4 tsp. salt
Freshly ground black pepper
3 lbs. sirloin or eye of round roast

1-1/2 cups red wine
2 Tbs. olive oil or vegetable oil
5 cloves garlic
12 large mushrooms, finely chopped
1 tsp. lemon juice
1/2 lb. bacon
1/2 cup beef broth
3 Tbs. flour

Place carrots, 1 onion finely chopped, bay leaf, thyme, parsley, salt, and pepper in a bowl. Add beef and wine. Cover and marinate the beef in the refrigerator for 24 hours, turning beef every 8 hours. Preheat oven to 350°. Remove meat and dry on paper towels. Strain and reserve marinade. Heat oil in a heavy flameproof casserole and brown meat on all sides over high heat. Reduce heat to medium and cook remaining onions and garlic in the same casserole for 3 minutes. Add mushrooms and lemon juice and continue cooking for 5 minutes, stirring frequently. At the same time, place bacon in a pan with 1 cup water and bring to a boil. Cook bacon for 5 minutes; drain bacon and cut into small pieces. Add beef broth to reserved marinade and heat to a simmer. Stir flour into onions and mushrooms. Add bacon. Replace beef in casserole and stir in warm wine and broth. Cover and cook 2-1/2 hours in preheated oven. Slice and serve.

4-6 servings

Gigot à la Moutarde

ROAST LEG OF LAMB WITH MUSTARD

1/2 cup Dijon mustard
2 Tbs. soy sauce
2 cloves garlic, crushed
1 tsp. ground thyme
1/4 tsp. powdered ginger
2 Tbs. olive oil
3-lb. boneless leg of lamb, rolled and tied

Preheat oven to 350°. Blend mustard, soy sauce, garlic, and ginger in a bowl. Whisk in olive oil 1 or 2 drops at a time, to make a thick mixture. Brush surface of lamb with mixture and set lamb on a rack in a roasting pan. Roast in preheated oven, allowing 1 to 1-1/4 hours for medium rare; or 1-1/4 to 1-1/2 hours for well done.

4-6 servings

Mousse au Chocolat

CHOCOLATE MOUSSE

Pinch salt
1 oz. (1 square) unsweetened chocolate
6-oz. package chocolate chips
5 eggs, separated
1/3 cup sugar
1/8 tsp. vanilla
1/2 pint heavy cream, whipped

Place a pinch of salt on the square of chocolate and melt it in a double boiler over simmering water. Add chocolate chips and melt them as well. Beat egg yolks lightly, and stir into chocolate. Heat several minutes, stirring constantly, and do not allow mixture to come to a boil. Add sugar and vanilla, and stir until sugar has mixed completely with chocolate. Allow a few minutes to cool. Beat egg whites until stiff, and fold in. Fold in whipped cream. Chill overnight.

6-8 servings

Poires au Vin Rouge

PEARS IN RED WINE

1 lb. ripe pears, peeled, halved, and cored
1 cup cold water with 1/2 Tbs. fresh lemon juice
1 cup red wine, preferably Bordeaux
Zest of 1/2 lemon
1/2 Tbs. fresh lemon juice
1/4 cup sugar
2 Tbs. honey
1/2 stick cinnamon
1 pinch nutmeg

Place halved pears in water and lemon solution to keep pears from discoloring. Combine wine and all other ingredients, and bring to a boil. Reduce heat to low. Let pears drain, add them to wine mixture, and cook on low heat for 8-10 minutes. Remove from heat and serve when cooled.

3-4 servings

Note: This simple and elegant dessert can be made well ahead of time and stored in the refrigerator.

Crème Pâtissière

Pastry Cream

1 pint whole milk
1 vanilla bean or 1 Tbs. vanilla extract
4 egg yolks
3/4 cup sugar
1/2 cup plus 2 Tbs. flour

Bring milk and vanilla to a boil and remove from heat. Blend egg yolks and sugar until ribbons form. Add flour slowly to egg and sugar mixture and blend to achieve a smooth texture. Add hot milk, a little at a time, to egg mixture, stirring constantly. Place pan back on heat and cook until mixture has thickened and flour is completely dissolved. Remove from heat and let cool.

1 pint

Fruits de la Saison Gratin

FRESH FRUIT GRATIN WITH PASTRY CREAM

3/4 cup whipping cream
1/8 cup sugar
3/4 cup crème pâtissière (see p. 58)
2 Tbs. orange-flavored liqueur
Seasonal fresh fruit, peeled, pitted, sliced, or cubed (enough for 6 servings)

Preheat oven to 350°. Whip cream with sugar. Gently mix the crème pâtissière, 2 tablespoons whipped cream, and liqueur. Using a metal spoon, gently fold in remaining cream. Arrange fruit in a pie pan, spoon over topping and bake 10 minutes in preheated oven. Transfer to a hot broiler, and allow top to crisp until brown. Serve immediately.

6 servings

Gâteau au Chocolat

MOLTEN CHOCOLATE CAKE

12 oz. French or Belgian bittersweet chocolate
1 cup butter
1 cup sugar
2 Tbs. all-purpose flour
5 eggs, separated

Preheat oven to 350°. Lightly grease 10-inch spring form pan and set aside. Melt chocolate and butter in top of double boiler over simmering water and remove from heat. Mix sugar, flour, and egg yolks in a bowl. Add to chocolate mixture and mix thoroughly. Beat egg whites to make soft peaks and fold gently into batter. Pour into prepared pan and bake in preheated oven 30 minutes. Cool in pan on rack. Remove outside of pan and place cake, on bottom of pan, on a serving plate. Serve warm, if possible.

10 servings

Delphine Vaucanson
Elizabeth Poyet

Crêpes

2 cups all-purpose flour
1 egg
1 Tbs. oil
1 Tbs. sugar
1/4 Tbs. vanilla extract
1/4 tsp. salt
2-1/2 cups whole milk

Place flour in electric mixer bowl. Add egg, oil, sugar, vanilla, and salt. Run mixer and pour the milk in slowly, and continue until batter is thoroughly mixed. Wait 30 minutes at least before cooking, if possible. Oil bottom of a 6- to 7-inch crêpe pan and place over high heat. When pan is hot, remove it from the heat and pour 1/4 cup batter into pan, moving pan around to distribute batter evenly. After a minute or so back over heat the crêpe should be cooked on that side and you may turn it and cook for another minute. Serve immediately.

If crêpes are to be used later, interleaf with waxed paper to prevent drying.

12-15 crêpes

Crêpes Suzette

BUTTER MIXTURE:
1 lb. unsalted butter, softened
1 lb. fine sugar
Grated rind of 1 orange
Grated rind of 1 lemon
2/3 cup orange juice

Cream butter with sugar; add remaining ingredients and mix well. Set aside in refrigerator until ready to use.

Butter mixture (above)	*2 tsp. fine sugar*
4 oz. Curaçao	*1/2 tsp. lemon juice*
Crêpes recipe (p. 61)	*4 oz. warm brandy*

Melt butter mixture in skillet of chafing dish. Add Curaçao and half of crêpes. Fold crêpes in halves, then quarters. Push to side of pan and repeat with remaining crêpes. Simmer 15 minutes. Sprinkle with sugar and lemon juice. Add brandy, light, and serve while blazing.

4 servings

Gâteau Normand

NORMANDY STYLE APPLE PIE

1 unbaked pastry shell
4 cups applesauce
1/3 cup sugar
2 Tbs. Calvados
1 package unflavored gelatin
4 Cortland apples, peeled, cored, and sliced thin
5 Tbs. sugar
2 Tbs. fresh lemon juice
1 Tbs. butter
1/2 cup plus 1 Tbs. apricot preserves, heated and strained

Preheat oven to 400°. Fit pastry shell into a 9-inch pie plate. Prick with a fork and bake in a preheated oven for 15 minutes; remove from oven. Reduce oven setting to 350°. Place applesauce, sugar, and Calvados in a small pan. Cook over moderate heat for 15 minutes until thick, stirring frequently. Dissolve gelatin in 1/3 cup water, heating slightly. Stir gelatin into applesauce mixture and fill pastry shell with mixture. Cover applesauce with apple slices. Sprinkle with sugar and lemon juice and dot with butter. Bake in preheated oven for 30 minutes. After baking, brush apples with strained apricot preserves.

8 servings

Soufflé Grand Marnier

5 Tbs. crème pâtissière (see p. 58)
2 egg yolks
2 Tbs. Grand Marnier
4 egg whites
2 Tbs. sugar
1 pinch salt

Preheat oven to 475°. Butter 2 ramekins (4-inch size) and dust them with sugar. Mix crème pâtissière and egg yolks thoroughly in a bowl. Add Grand Marnier and mix thoroughly. Whip egg whites to stiff peaks in another bowl, and fold in sugar and a pinch of salt (or, if you wish, add sugar before whipping). Fold egg whites gently into the mixture, one-third at a time. Pour soufflé batter into the 2 ramekins and bake in preheated oven for about 12 minutes.

2 servings

Image Credits

Cover Image, p. 4: *Still-Life, Apples and Oranges*, Paul Cézanne, ca. 1890, Musée d'Orsay
© Edimédia/CORBIS

p. 9: *Montmarte*, François Gall, Bass Museum of Art © Bass Museum of Art/CORBIS

pp. 10, 59: *Still Life With a Basket*, Paul Cézanne, ca. 1888-1890, Musée d'Orsay
© Archivo Iconografico, S.A./CORBIS

p. 19: *Boulevard Montmartre, Afternoon Sun, Spring 1897*, Camille Pissarro,
Jerusalem Museum © AFP/CORBIS

pp. 24, 41: *Cafe Terrace at Night*, Vincent van Gogh, ca. 1888, Rijksmuseum Kroller-Muller
© Francis G. Mayer/CORBIS

pp. 35, 45: *The Luncheon of the Boating Party*, Pierre-Auguste Renoir, ca. 1881,
Phillips Collection © Francis G. Mayer/CORBIS

p. 38: *The Eiffel Tower*, Raoul Dufy, ca. 1935, Private collection © Edimédia/CORBIS

pp. 21, 49: *The Lunch*, Claude Monet, 1873-1874, Musée d'Orsay
© Archivo Iconografico, S.A./CORBIS

p. 55: *At Pere Lathuille's*, Edouard Manet, 1879, Musée des Beaux-Arts
© Archivo Iconografico, S.A./CORBIS

Table for Two in Paris

CD Playlist

1. LA MER (Trenet) Charles Trenet

2. QUE RESTE-T-IL DE NOS AMOURS (Trenet/Chauliac) Charles Trenet

3. LA VIE EN ROSE (Louiguy/Piaf) Edith Piaf

4. MÉNILMONTANT (Trenet) Charles Trenet

5. DOUCE JOIE (Viseur) Gus Viseur

6. LA ROMANCE DE PARIS (Trenet) Charles Trenet

7. PARLEZ-MOI D'AMOUR (Lenoir) Lucienne Boyer

8. IMAGINEZ (Midway/Poterat) Charles Trenet

9. CAPRICE MUSETTE (Colombo) Tony Murena

10. UN AIR QUI VIENT DE CHEZ NOUS (Trenet) Charles Trenet

11. C'ETAIT UNE HISTOIRE D'AMOUR (Contet/Jeanjal) Edith Piaf

12. FEU DE BOIS (Wal Berg/Amade) Yves Montand

13. PRÈS DE TOI MON AMOUR (Trenet/Luypaerts) Charles Trenet

14. FLÂNER TOUS LES DEUX (Misraki/Hornez/Coquatrix) Yves Montand